From the Sandpiles of My Mind

Ralph M. Zeigler

PublishAmerica
Baltimore

First printing

ISBN: 1-4137-5087-7
PUBLISHED BY PUBLISHAMERICA, LLLP
www.publishamerica.com
Baltimore

Printed in the United States of America

FOREWORD

All characters in this book are fictitious. My choice of subjects and characters has been limited only to the extent of my imagination.

I wish to thank my daughter Jennifer Jo for her ceaseless work in helping me to assemble these two volumes and presenting them for publication.

From my association with various poets writing groups such as ISP, Lebanon Writer's Moscow Idaho, Palouse Cowboy Association, Moscow Choral Group I received a wealth of demand and encouragement. Priceless was the encouragement I received from my family especially my English War Bride, Betty, and my Indian wife, Irma.

I am grateful that God has allowed me nearly a century in which to express myself; endowed me with "the gift of gab" and a verse writer's talent to present to the reader a few hours of pleasant reading.

Ralph M. Zeigler

Sandpiles of the Mind

The fingers of my senses stir
The sand piles of my mind
Thru them trickle words and thoughts
Things now left behind.

They clutch at bits of memory
That swiftly through them flow
Recalling bits of happiness
Before I let them go.

I am very thankful
That God has been so kind
And willed this final blessing
The sand pile of the mind.

BOYHOOD AND NATURE

He Won't Dare

Me 'N Billy had a fight
'Bout my Dad
'N it was sad
He said that he
Was stupid, see
Mostly he was right.

'M gonna get a great big Dane
With snarl and growl
'N eerie howl
'N chewed up ears
That Billy fears
'N collar 'n a chain.

I'll take my dog up to his door
'N he will see
What I've with me
We'll take a walk
But he wont talk
'Bout my Daddy anymore.

Jimmy and My Marbles

I'm awfully good at "Mumbly-peg"
Jimmy, he is better
I throw a ball, high on the wall
Jimmy hits a letter.

Jimmy hit me in the nose
Coz of what I said
Jimmy tried to tear my shirt
Tore my cap instead.

Jimmy's got my marbles
In his marble sack
Wish'n I was Joe Louis
I'd get my marbles back.

Old Testament and Peanut Butter

As a boy I found much joy
In food both sweet and sour
It was gold both hot and cold
I ate at any hour.
The taste of fruit, of licorice root
Berries from the vine
Oyster stew, catsup too
Were like the taste of wine.

The stories told of men of old,
Joseph, Samuel, Saul,
Job and Jonah, Isaac, Noah,
I loved to read them all.
I felt the swing of David's sling
The jaw bone of the Ass
I always knew that they were true
But time can change, alas.

Food has lost its savor
Those tastes that I recall,
And all that's told of men of old
I scarce believe at all.

Ode to the Thunder Mug

The treasured pot was really not
The one you cooked the stew in
It sat instead beneath the bed
The one we always peed in.

The lid it fit and you could sit.
On a winter night
When you were scared to go half bared
To sit a hole in fright.

That gurgling fool the modern stool
That sits there in plain sight
Lacks honesty, the modesty
It lacks the circle bite.

Twill ne'er replace the potty's Grace
In winter's dead of night.

For Me It's Hand-Me-Downs

From two to twelve its true you know
Things don't outwear, they just outgrow
If there's a cousin within in bounds
You'll sure be blessed with hand-me-downs.

I seemed to fit in by some chance
I never had a pair of pants
In all the time I'd ever known
That some one else had not out grown.

Even Sis had willed to me
Shirts and sox since I was three
In all my life I'd never worn
A garment that had not been torn.

When I was ten, I worked real hard
Helping Mother render lard
As a reward she purchased me
The first new pants since I was three.

As we were leaving from the store
I slipped and snagged them on the door
The next day I got in a fight
When I got home, they were a sight.

So now I go my usual rounds
I even wear my hand-me-downs.

Putting an Edge On

The razor strap hung on the door
And dangled down toward the floor
Dad would get his old straight edge
From its place on chimney ledge
From movements swift the blade grew keen
The sharpest edge I've ever seen
That strap sure put an edge on.

When we had quarreled or maybe fought
Swore or sassed or things forgot
Dad unhooked the razor strap
And we could feel the leather slap
As we were bended over knee
It really honed our memory
That strap sure put the edge on.

The days of razor strap are gone
Remembered just in verse and song
I've found myself another tool
To keep me so I'm not a fool
A shelf of books has come to be
What the strap was once to me
They really put an edge on.

Forgiveness

Aunty caught me swearing
Washed my mouth with soap
Snatched me from the busy street
Tied me with a rope.
Stopped my fight with Billy
Sent me straight to bed
I tore her dress, pulled her hair
Wished that she were dead.
It was very late at night
I woke up with a start
To find myself in darkness
Pressed to Auntie's heart.

Contemplations on a Crapper

On such a throne Queens, Kings have sat
Vicars, Merchants and Vagrants
Here Virgins did their daily chores
Students, Teachers, Nuns and Whores
Even simple souls like me
A throne of true Democracy.
Pity the souls who sadly rue it
Wouldn't say Shit but still have to do it.

Pink Packet Philosophy

That special sweetness that you bring
With my morning cup
Stirs my sluggish plugged up veins
Each morning wakes me up
Would that I were half my age
And you a few years older
I'd wear my heart upon my sleeve
And be a little bolder.
Were I again a handsome youth
I might turn quite judicial
And wonder if like packet sweet
Your charm was artificial.

Infatuation

The Gods had adjudged it was never to be
But everything 'bout her kept calling to me
The way she talked or smiled, her laugh
Her tight little breasts, her well molded calf
For the touch of her hand each time she passed by
I would live a fantasy, dream a lie.
Now she has vanished like all the rest.
And I know in my heart, it is for the best.

Like Father, Like Son

Dad hasn't given us the right
To leave the table yet
He talks and talks
Or maybe walks
To stove or telephone.

We're not allowed to speak or fight
Or cat or puppy pet
Or hum, or sing
Or anything
Even when alone.

Some day I'll have a family
Much as seven yet
I'll make them stay
While I go 'way
Because when I am grown,
I'LL BE THE GROWNUP

Unscrambling the Scrammed

My brain is in a terrible knot
For I forget what I forgot
An I've forgot what I forget
Forget forgot, I'll get it yet
Or not undo this knotty knot
Don't laugh—the truth is truly true
The same could happen too to you

Blank Verse

If punctuation drives you nuts
And lengthy phrases end in buts
Thus you have trouble writing prose
Strike words and phrases here and there
Rearrange the rest with care
You don't need rhythm to the line
No one couplet has to rhyme
BY GOSH!! BEFORE YOU KNOW IT
YOU'VE ARRIVED—YOU ARE A POET!!

Modern Verse

The more I read
It makes sense
If you would write
Condense, condense
For we compose
For college Grads
Whose reading span
Is TV ADS

Advice for Contentment

I strolled last night with the ghost of my youth
On a sandy Moon lit shore
We spoke of all the dreams of the past
That was part of the dreams of yore
I thought to myself "If I had back the youth
With the knowledge I have today.
I could surmount the greatest of heights
That—by chance might come my way"

At once the Ghost quickened his steps
I soon fell far behind
He turned and watched my labored approach
He seemed to be reading my mind
He took me gently by the hand
And said, "That is not our God's way
So just be thankful at your age
For what you have today."

A Million Miles from Home

I walk in the early morning, in the gently falling rain
When in the pit of my stomach I feel this stirring pain
It could just as well be nowhere, a long long mile from home

Why did I take that physic, I could have left it to chance
Oh Lord that horrible feeling, you might dirty your pants
It could just as well be nowhere, 3/4 a mile to home

I look for a bridge, or bushes, a steep bank by a stream
My bowels give a sudden rumble, almost make me scream
It could just as well be nowhere, 1/2 a mile to home.

Now I'm walking knock kneed, walking like I'm on ice
The thought of what might happen isn't' very nice
I could just as well be nowhere, 1/4 of mile to home

I make it through the kitchen my coat left on the floor
Desperately tour the hall to a locked bathroom door
I could just as well be nowhere, I do not make it home

Aging—Reminiscing

In the wee hours of the morning
While the rest were soundly sleeping
Sat this old man in his rocker
Sat with pain of indigestion
Bones a creek with Arthritis
Bitterly he cursed the nagging nature
Of his many sore afflictions

Then the gently rocking motion
Brought to him at last some comfort
Half asleep he started dreaming
Of the active days of boyhood
Of his glorious days of manhood
Of his days of love and courtship
Of the love of wife and children
Of a third new generation

Thus he wakened to the present
To the world of indigestion
To this world of arthritis
Now he sat in contemplation
Of his many many blessings
Thankful for his low blood pressure
Thankful for no sign of cancer
Thanked his God to be alive

In this world at Eighty five
As he counts his many blessings
He'll not think of yesterday
But of his wife soundly sleeping
In their bed not far away.

Dreams on a Winter Day

I hear a familiar Clip, Clop, Clip, Clop
This Clip, Clop does not ever stop
It's a horse a walking on the brick
Of a city street where the ice is thick
The horse sharp shod for the winter's day
And steady he goes on his way.

A lone train whistle far far away
A haunting sound in the breaking day
As freight cars hurrying on their way
Each rail end clicks to the passing cars
Caboose lights twinkle back at the stars

A pheasant calls upon the hill
The air is heavy, the morning still
He's out with first light to get his fill
His colors are bright in the morning light
Before he ducks and is out of sight

I'm oncc again a bare foot lad
Filled with dreams and OH so Glad!
Then suddenly I am very sad
For today I'm old and tired and grey
Just dreaming sounds of another day

Computeritis

I wake in the night in a cold sweat
A victim of that virus
This is known in the modern world
As congenitive conputeritis
I rise in the night in the early hour gloom
And make my way to my computer room
I click on the light and sit on my chair
For awhile at the blank monitor I stare
With a mouse neath my hand, I'm on my way
To the computer world before break of day

Then pushing a few buttons I soon connect
To the amazing world of the Internet
First thing I check is my "Email"
Then scan the Net for the latest sale
Four hours later it starts to get light
I've been on the Internet most of the night
Forgotten each day are TV and papers
As I surf the Net for the latest capers
I wonder if some day I'll regret
Succumbing to the Internet
At present I welcome this strange new virus
That is known in the world as congentitiv conputeritis!

The Vacant Chair

A rocker filled with memories
Softly rocks in the evening breeze
Its arms once held Ann's curly locks
Suffering from the Chicken Pox
Here Mother rocked her babies three
Daddy nursed an injured knee
With movement slight it's heard to speak
Oh rocker moved by evening breeze
Brings back a host of memories

Scents from the Scrapbook of the Minds

The smell of chalk in a school room
And that fresh polish on the shoes
Mingle with the damp of wet clothing
And ink smell from the news
Suddenly the smells of the garden
Fresh flowers and vegetables there
Then old harnesses and English leather
Fresh mown grass everywhere
Odors of horses and cattle
Acrid smell of fresh milk
Plum and apply blossom
And that of a skating rink
The smell of bacon frying
And that of fresh baked bread
The scent of her unique perfume
As she lay asleep on the bed
The old man sits there dreaming
With age he's both deaf and blind
As a world of smells and odors
Drift gently through his mind

Creation or Womb

I did not ask to be there; neither did they
Where there was no night; there was no day
In that meaningless void, closed in tight
I was in them and they were in me
Like that long age time, in that long ago sea
Before the day of fish or dove
Before the day of hate and love
The only sound heard by them or by me
Was the sound of the waves of the restless sea
As we all struggled there just to be
When done—but one—only me
Alive, alive, floating free
Thus I wakened but not in alarm
Sweat drenched but exceedingly calm
Hunger lips sought soothing breast
As I joined the world of all the rest
Now I am confused in this mind of mine
Could I have been there at that beginning of time
Or just at the creation of body and mind?

Clouds

Floating gently into view
Mysteries to me and you

Casting shadows o'er the ground
Ever changing without sound

Hiding morning's sunshine rays
Bringing gloom, perhaps for days

Slipping softly o'er the moon
Bring peaceful rest at noon

Never making any noise
Though they bring us tears or joys
Clouds.

A little ship loose at sea
High in heaven do I see

Into sight soon drifts another
It is followed by a brother

Little ships with masts asail
Coasting high o'er hill and vale

Painting beauty in the sky
Never pausing, passing by

Vanishing from our sight at last
Like our thoughts into the past
Clouds.

Billowing bluffs from the west
Rising up to puff its chest

Yet fleecy trimming falsifies
The bluff it threatens in the skies

As with grumbling it passes
Leaving yet a sky of blue

Makes heart leap with joy anew
Thunderheads thus pass us by
Those who wished for rain may sigh
Clouds cont.

Waking up some morn let's say
We face a dark and dismal day

Water dripping from the eave
Spring's bright sunshine is on leave

Gray and shadowy floating lace
Swiftly, drifting fore wind's pace

Drenching earth and chilling air
Water, dampness every where

But it wakes the grass anew
Flowers too so don't be blue
Clouds.

Bring rain, snow and sleet
Natures guard from frost and heat

Helping pain the sunset bright
Floating ghostlings in the night

Hiding moon, bringing kisses
To our spooning love sick Misses

Fortune tellers of the sky
Mysteries sweet to you and I
Clouds.

Fare Well

Here on this lonely cliff top
Facing the wind and the sea
I recall many trips to this beach side
And what they have meant to me.

How I loved those walks of a morning
With the crunch of the still wet sand
The voice of the restless ocean
And flotsam on every hand.

How I thrilled to the panorama
That colored the morning sky
The sun's first rays on the surf spray
The sea gull's haunting cry

I watched you asleep on the soft sand
At the edge of the shade from the bluff
Hoping to get a sun tan
But only just enough.

Those gold summer twilights
After watching the setting sun
The calm receding ocean
And the end of a day of fun.

How I've loved those walks in this setting
By the every murmuring sea
I wonder if even God knows
What they have meant to me.

I watch—The wind stirs sand clouds
And hurries them along
Is this fare well to this beach side
And the days when we both were strong?

Adios

The rustling leaves, their color faded
Clung to the stately trees
Active squirrels with bushy plumes
Seemed shy and ill at ease.

The sun had lost its summer heat
Was now content to bless
Homeward children dawdling 'long
With one last soft caress.

Amongst the clouds familiar "V's"
Of wild fowl cruised the sky
And it was Autumn once again
I grieved, I know not why.

A Melody of Shapes and Sounds

Sweet the sound of Meadow Lark
A song that sounds so dear
Lilting song of little brook
Brings happiness and cheer
Spring Glorious Spring

Forget the cold of winter
Snow-storms wild
Feast eye upon new emerald green
And Dandelions of gold
Spring Glorious Spring

Busy buzzing of Machines
Buzzing busy Bee on knoll
Add to the Melody of Spring
Enhancing mind and soul
A mute song of Spring
SPRING! GLORIOUS SPRING!

Magic Dream

A boy/who once/ believed/ in mag/ic Dream
One day/set forth/to spark/ling brook/ to play
And there/ in sun/lits Gold/en spark/ling stream
The Fair/y folk/, a host/, had come/ to play

The birds/the bees/and ev/en fish/and trees
A gath/erd crowd/ to see/a vast/ array
Of glist/ning wings/ until/ a stir/ring breeze
Did make /these tin/y creat/ures fade /away

Then bird/ and bee/and tree/at once /quiet grew
As shad/ows formed/upon/now dark/end nook
The boy/his faith/ in Fair/ies now/ renewed
Arose/ and took/one long/ and part/ing look

I say/I saw/though oth/ers say/it was/ a dream
Say fair/ies cant/ be seen/in shad/y glens
But for/ the kind/that rid/i/cule the name
In fantacy/you know/true ones/appear/ to men

The Solitary Watcher

He waits there for the night to come
Watches the slowly setting sun
Silhouetted against the sky
He hears the sea gulls lonely cry
And the receding surf tide's sigh

He looks upon the shifting sands
Where once he dreamed of other lands
The day recedes into the night
The Evening star becomes alight

Where are those dreams of yesterday?
One last look, one last dream

He turns away

A Home Is Not a Home Without a Garden

In a flat, facing factories, she raised her little brood
They were known in the district as a happy family
Little cherubs, little blossoms, Meg and Jude and Emily
Were these flower that were nurtured, in health and with food

Black as Black Onyx were the tresses, of sweet Meg and laughing Judy
Carrot colored were the ringlets of the darling Emily
There was not another garden quite as full of grace and color
As these girls in flowered gingham, made by hand by the mother

Their whispers were like summer breezes, laughter like a brook o'er rocks
Strong and sturdy as the Sunflowers, pretty as the Hollyhocks
In time and in full blossom, each were wooed and wed
They brought forth their fruit by bearing, Tim and Jan and Ned

Garden keepers like no others
Were these lovely little mothers
Trained by a master gardener

Note: The black onyx is not black in its natural state but is dyed and takes on a high polish. The choice of this color and that of carrot was one of the most difficult choices I had to make. .

Confusion

It's Springtime in the Autumn
I'm sure confused with this
It's like Able slaying brother Cain
Eve stealing the serpent's kiss
The sun shines bright at midnight
The Moon is out all day
I feed my cows my breakfast
And contentedly munch their hay
My chickens grow in my garden
And my vegetables daily lay
Fresh fruit in the hen nests
My cider has turned to whey
My wine has turned to water
Jonah swallows a whale
A whole darned city reappears
As result of a hurricane gale

"Honey", she says". You've been dreaming"
I come back to Earth once more
With my feet upon my pillow
And my noggin on the floor
It's getting close to daylight
Finally I awake
Have six shots of Scotch for breakfast
And go fish for birds in the lake

Oh Glorious Spring

Shed your fur cap and your mittens
As with sunshine you are smitten
Change the snow tires on your auto
The oil too, you really aught to
Your summer tires have worn too thin
They'll have to be replaced again
Oh Glorious Spring

Paint on your house looks a sight
Your summer pants have grown too tight
Your summer straw hat looks a fright
Your bedroom is too warm at night
Oh Glorious Spring

Its time—into your garden go
Prepare the ground for seed to sow
Set out small plants row by row
That night you hear the North wind blow
Temperature killing frost and snow
Oh Glorious Spring

Determined, you replant again
To see the small plants drenched with rain
The soil is mud up to your knees
You feel a chill and start to sneeze
So—in to your bed you go

While pesky weeds start to grow
And smother out the plants your know
Oh Glorious Spring

LOVE AND FAMILY

Infatuation? Affection? Love?

Where do we go from here Luv
Where do we go from here?
We who were strangers a short time ago
Where do we go from here?

Where does it go from here Luv
For a woman of marital strife
With one who proved unfaithful
And another who took his life.
Left with a doubt of sincerity
That man has for a wife.

Where does it go from here Luv
With a man not healed from the pain
A man who may never release the past
Be unable to love again?
Needing that tender affection
To help him reduce the pain?

Where do we go form here Luv
With a man who is hesitant to
Accept the tender min-strations
Of one understanding as you
We must not hurt one another
Yet as each of us need a change
Time may heal us yet Luv
Both of us love again.

Where do we go from her Luv
Life's answers are sometimes tough
So lets share from what we have Luv
For now lets hope its enough.

The Blessing That Fate Bestows

Oh the blessing that fate bestow
On some of us as we older grow
Some wonderful one we come to know
That brightens our life in its afterglow

Spawned by a look, a certain style
A few shared thoughts, a friendly smile
Cupid lured us with his wile
And love was budding all the while.

We shared the thoughts that made life dear
Expressing our bad side without fear
The tearful moments, our times of cheer
That love might grow as we grow nearer

Let's relish for now with love held out
Kiss away each tear or doubt
If by chance it won't work out
May we always cherish what this is about:

A WONDERFUL CHANCE FOR CONTENTMENT

Sal

I sat alone this afternoon
Old Pal
And wonder how things were for you
And Sal
I love her still though you have won
Her Heart
And that is why we must remain forever
Now apart
Never while this heart of mine
Feels thus
Will I return, I'll do what's best
For us
They say that God is fair and just
Old Pal
I hope he takes good care of you
And Sal.

The First Quarrel

He really hadn't meant to say
What he had in quite that way
It had sounded very strong
And she had up and took it wrong
So they had a little fight
Love settled it before the night

AND BOTH SAID THEY WERE SORRY

Another Quarrel

She sits there looking at the sea
Damn his stupid pride
He's really half the man that she
Expected as a bride
He kicks the sand beneath his feet

And curses that one day
He took her as a bride so sweet
She sure don't act that way
Evenings after very little is said
And they are sleeping back to back
When finally in the bed

Final Quarrel

She throws the ring upon the floor
And stamps upon the stone
The whole affair is breaking up
He feels it in his bones
He takes a step toward her
Hate shining in his eyes
She draws back in sudden fear
She bows her head and cries

HE LOOKS—HE TURNS—HE LEAVES HER

Late that night upon the street
Far from their flat they chance to meet
She mutely holds up fingered ring
He clasps his hand upon this thing
They need not talk—there's ought to tell
Love settles all—ALL IS WELL

What Is Love?

Love is the Angel Dust
That settles on our lives
A little gift that GOD bestows
To make us realize

THERE IS A HEAVEN

Falling in Love Late in Life

It's all too easy to fall in love
It's all to easy to find a mate
But once you've joined it becomes a task
To take that love and make it last

There is a sudden change from what you've known
As time has passed you both have grown
Quite content with the way
You've lived your life day by day

Like different grapes from different vines
Tend to result in different wines
Mix the two and in the end
It's very important how they blend

A Bit of a Quarrel

No stereo—No T.V.
No sound of kettle set for tea
Silence—Silence save for rustle
Of evening paper

Silence—Charged silence
While Love hovers restless
In the wings

He recedes to slumber
Quietly she covers him
With a soft blanket
And a mantle of love

What Part of You Do I Like the Most?

You ask what part of you I like the best
I like your patience and your willingness to share
I like the little ways you show you care
I like to hear the tinkle of your laughter on the phone
Or watch you when you think you're all alone
I like the way you treat my family
And how you shine when out in company

I like the snow white softness of your ample breasts
I love to snuggle into them, caress and rest
I love your kisses 'specially deep ones
As my exploring hands encase your buns
I like to catch you as you leave the shower
So warm so soft I would I could devour

I love in bed when we both recline
And I embrace this miracle that's mine
Responding to our need—desire
Our sexual passions fill us both with fire
I like to make you make that passion noise
That shows how much my efforts you enjoy
Till thus our passion have been satiated to the core
We lie in embrace satisfied once more

You ask what part of you I like the best
Its like choosing from all food I like the best
Or choosing my best poem from all the rest
Or choosing one star from the nightly glow
Or choosing which way I would have the wind to blow

Adventures in Parenting

A winding cow path led the way
To that special knoll
That had its top removed
And thus create a hole
Where sand and gravel were removed to mix into cement
That went to build foundations
Or floor for basement went

'Twas in this little sheltered place
With a neighbor girl I'd play
We two would make like Mom and Dad
Act in a family way
But sister Sue spied on us
Couldn't wait to tell
What she told our families
Caused all kinds of hell

But when it all was sorted out
They sure could not blame me
For I was only twelve years old
And she was twenty three

Was Cupid Only Fooling?

Was it love that inspired her
Or was it a whim
Or maybe
Just maybe
She mistook him for Jim
Twas Dolly that kissed him
That night long ago
Will she remember
He surely hopes so
He's to see tonight
So at last he will know

The First Kiss

A smell of roses
In the air
She approached him
Standing there
He felt her warm hands
On his neck
She gave his cheek
A little peck

Was it Love?
Did she care?
She kissed and left
Him standing there

His mind in turmoil
His face ablaze
Blushing at his thoughts
For days
Infatuation
Has its ways

She'd just left him
standing there
Did she love him?
Did she care?

They met again
Another day

She gave one glance
And turned away
She did not speak
What could he say?

Had she loved him?
Had she cared?
Or had she kissed him
To win a dare?

A Nugget of Knowledge

We walked the fields with Grampa
Eight abreast, a full four span
Pulling weeds from growing grain
A job for boy and man.

Grampa paired us man and boy
He'd often tell us all
"One boy's a boy, two boys a half
And three, no boy at all."

He'd often take one of us out
To help replace the corn
That did not grow or pheasants got
For two he showed his scorn.

For Gramps adhered to his belief
His wisdom I recall
"one boy's a boy, two's a half
And three no boy at all."

'Bye for Now, Luv

There's this one last look at your picture
Before I take it down
Like memories, it's starting to fade dear
The edges are turning brown

I know as I tenderly wrap it
Before I put it away
Twill always be part of my past dear
Like the memories I have today

I pray in my heart you forgive dear
As now I seek a new wife
T'was our wonderful years together
That inspires me to seek a new life

Last Time Leaving Home

Trees and roses are untrimmed
A job for February snow
The flower beds are just a mess
Work needed long ago

Paint is peeling on the fence
Dandelions dot the lawn
A sad expression of our dreams
Now that you are gone.

That little seedling that we set
Is now a towering tree
As are the ones we set for hedge
Your privacy to please.

Though faint, the path that Heidi took
Can still be traced around
To where you sunbathed in the sun
To reach a gold brown.

The screen and porch roof but remind
Of Tisha standing there
Calling me to fetch her down
And smooth her ruffled hair.

Here's the place of garbage cans
Where Dinah used to stand
A challenge to the Garbage man
As he came for the cans.

I take this one last lonely tour
Then slowly drive away
From tears, and years of happiness
I sold the house today.

The Other Watch

Betty loved a bargain, be it great or small
From handkerchiefs to spats
Silverware to hats
Furniture to mats
She loved to shop for all.

She spurned the cheap made thing.
Woods and metal knew
Chinaware too
What color was for you
From cloth to toy to ring.

Precious things I'd never get.
I'd let her shop for days
Exercising ways
To win a shopper's praise
I'd just wait and write the check.

This wristwatch was a prize.
The works a little old
The band 12 Karat gold
I knew that she was sold
By the sparkle in her eyes.

She had this watch for years.
Though the band was stout
The works kept slipping out
While we searched about
She'd almost be in tears.

It disappeared one day
Bet was in a trance
But by some lucky chance
She found it in her pants
Things like that are odd that way.

The works were finally lost at last
Today while going through
Things both old and new
That has she left for you
I found that empty band to the past.

Modern Living

We'd go for a walk when the day was done
Pause to watch the setting sun
Water the flowers, bush and vine
Bring in the clothes from off the line
Have a light snack a bit of tea
And settle down to watch T.V.
Watch the news; or "What's my Line"
And she would sip her glass of wine
When her eyes would tire, it was time
For a tape of Denver or Patsy Cline
I knew I was hers and she was mine.

Thanksgiving (Modern)

Out of this drive and by the gas pump
To our daughter's house we go
We need no oats for this bucket of bolts
We only hope it don't snow.
Out through the Boondocks and onto the Freeway
We put her to seventy and over
There's a horn's chilling blast as a trucker roars past
Forcing us onto the shoulder.
Through city streets and up the last hill
And finally into the drive
The battle is o'er we're safe at their door
Surprised that we're still alive
I make for the trees, my bladder to ease
Step on a slick board in the grass
I start to swear as my feet take the air
And I find myself flat on my ass.
The turkey is done, we have lots of fun
With piano and sing-song together
And finally retire with an electrical fire
That can't quite compete with the weather.
I don't try to kneel as the chill I feel
Instead I slip into bed
I turn to the wall and thank God for all
That's been done, and been had and been said.

U No Hu

He sits and ponders what to do
This funny old man at a 1/4 2 2
All he can think about right now is you
How you put on his socks and shoe
Without you to comfort him what would he do
Sometimes he wishes he were new
Had more umph for things we do
He may not be the best 'tis true
This funny old man called U NO HU

Hawaii

In that enchanted land
We strolled the sugar sand
The view was really grand
In Hawaii

A native climbs a tree
Picks a coconut for me
As I sat beside by the sea
In Hawaii

Then they played those haunting tunes
AS we sat beneath the moon
And ate food without our spoons
In Hawaii

Then a little native flirt
Barefoot in the dirt
Did a dance in a grass skirt
In Hawaii

As this little lass
Made each seductive pass
I dreamed of mowing grass
In Hawaii

Winning the Golden Spurs

At the tender of three
My rocking horse was dear to *me*
At the grown up age of four
I rode my broom stick horse to war
A curtain rod was my lance
And tin can armor on my pants
My sister had a kiddy car
She hit my stick horse with a jar
I found myself upon the floor
Decided I would ride no more
At ten I rode an aging mare
Around the farm, most everywhere
Until she trotted 'neath a tree
A low branch swept her from me
I lost my breath and hurt my knee
I swore that "Riding Aint for me"
But in my teens a Rodeo
Came to our town—put on a show
They advertised a Flea bit Roan
"If you can ride him, take him home"
Now things were tough upon the farm
I'd take a chance, 'twould do no harm
You guessed it, it was just my fate
I fell off 'fore he reached the gate
Now I am known as Cowboy Joe

I have my own T.V. show
I wear my Cowboy hat with pride
With Silver Pistols by my side
I stand there clad in Shirt and spur
And spread that old Cowboy Manure

86 and On Hold

I wake in the night with a cramp in my neck
I start for the bathroom a problem to check
In a tangle of bed clothes I fall from the bed
Tip over the night stand and land on my head
While escaping the bed clothes I smile with relief
For a week they've been lost my lower false teeth
I sit on the floor in contemplation
Of this process they call degeneration
I'm either suffering a diarrhea irritation
Or plagued with a week of constipation
I've a recurring pain in the small of by back
One knee gives away and my feet fail to track
The glasses I have do not fit my eyes
And because of my hearing I just sit looking wise
Any everyone thinks that I'm the town's sage
A living fossil of another age
The hair is long gone from the top of my head
Once muscular arms are no almost dead
My sing voice is a guttural mix
But I thank God I'm alive at 86

Ann's Logic

I was playing with her toy
I didn't mean to hurt it
She tried to snatch it away from me
Between us two, we broke it
She pulled my hair
I scratched her face
We had an awful fight
Mother sent us both upstairs
'Til it was almost night
It's winter time, it's cold outside
We're stuck inside together
So I don't think Sis likes either
Somehow we must end this fight
Someone must say, "I'm sorry."

Line Fences and Neighbors

Here once Line fences clearly drew
The boundary line of farms that we once knew
Where herd and herd pastured side by side
The Line fence there would separate-divide
Neighbors living side by side

Children gathered at the local school
To learn their sums and the Golden rule
This schoolhouse served yet a need
For neighbors then were separate breeds
They met in evenings when their work was done
For gossip, politics and fun.
From common cause great friendship grew
A neighbors thoughts a neighbor knew

Together neighbors threshed their grain
A death of one to all brought pain
When Uncle Joe broke his leg
The Neighbors shucked and stored his corn
A Neighbor girl kept house for us
When brother Fay was born

One did not ask from others pay
You might need them another day
Many times I've heard said,
"Many thanks 'til better paid"
But you could bet if help were dear
There was another neighbor near

Small farms and line fences have vanished
Giant farms continue on and on
Good fences do no more make good Neighbors
The fences and the Neighbors now are gone

At Eighty-Eight

In bed at half past seven
For me that's kind of late
But we have just one bathroom
And her appointment is at eight
I hear the front door closing
I rise to clean up and dress
Go down to get the latest
From the Daily Morning Press
The elevator takes my back
One more to my floor
To find that 'cause the wife insists
When I left I locked the door.
So I decide to go for a morning walk
A breakfast out alone
I sort of wander about the town
Until the wife shows up at home.
She says, "I thought you always check
For the keys you always keep
On a chain about your neck?

After lunch I hurry to change
For an appointment we have that day
At a local retirement home
Where we are supposed to play
As I sit to don my trousers
And sadly recall the day
When I could easily put them on
In the good old fashioned way

The wife says, “Why are you dressing?”
That appointment was yesterday.
I go down to check for the latest mail
Returning I cannot win
I have to ring the doorbell
I’d locked the door again
I’m not really absent minded
I’m just a slow learner!

HEALTH AND HOSPITAL

In the Presence of Darkness

I trod the halls of the critical ward
Or sat alone by her bed
Listened to the shallow breath
Or mumbled phrases said.
Across the hall a group was gathered
Speaking in a quiet tones
They too maintained a vigil
Of another in this zone.
I sensed a cold dark presence
Death had come to call
Was I wrong in thanking God
That it struck across the hall?

An Invitation to Eternity

I was hardly aware I was standing there
Birds sang sweet in the grass at my feet
To real to be but a dream
The sun went to rest at its home in the west
And the bird songs suddenly died
The earth suddenly gave, and an open grave
What a wonderful place to hide.

Hills Now Too Tall to Climb

I walk the level pathways
And view that other path
Leading up the hill
That I used to climb, alas.

I never reached the summit
And often when I'd stop
I'd tell myself "The day will come
I will reach the top."

Now, strolling level pathways
I often contemplate
How other goals have been forestalled
Success was left to fate.

Till now this tired old traveler
Surrenders them to time
Reflecting on those other goals
Hills now too tall to climb.

Pills, Pills, Pills

Some speed you up
Some slow you down
Keep you calm and sane
Its odd to me
They never composed
A pill to ease the pain
Of Taking Countless Pills

Inattention or Deafness?

"You're crazy; It's 'cause you mutter
My hearing's as good as the day
When we first got married
Even better I'd say;
So—
Don't shout!!—
My God!—
I hear you !!!!
(Now what in hell did she say.)

Victim of an Injury

I watch the messengers of doom
Creep from the corners of the room
Froze with fear I hold my breath
And wait the clammy cold of death
Relax—this useless bit of strife
Leads not to death but afterlife
That waits beyond.

Is not each sparrow's futile fall
Well within the Master's call?
If you have learned to love—forgive
You face this death but for to live
Though mortal dust is mixed with sod
The living souls returns to God
And joy Eternal.

Then, all at once I hear a shout
Sis has got the splinter out
"You'll live," She says.

From Hospital Notes

Men are born with one appendage
Two exposed glands and a cleavage
That are kept most carefully hidden
And rarely ever is it bidden
That they reveal, this little treasure
For anything but well planned pleasure.

If he's modest he may curse
The efficient, charming Prepping nurse
She doesn't laugh or gawk or play
She merely shaves the hair away
And if he felt exposed before
He'll feel it now More and MORE.

Army Night Nurse

She was blessed with a bountiful four feet beam
Her coiffure was tangled and thatched
With breastwork ample for ten to feed
And size 12 feet that matched.

Her mouth was always packed with gum
She chewed it like a cud
When people asked as they always did
She insisted her name was “Spud.”

She never announced her coming
She merely loomed into view
That was probably just as well
For her voice scared the hell out of you.

Yet she never complained if a sheet was twice soiled
She was thorough yet gentle too
And wasn’t afraid to challenge
If she thought it best for you.

Her patients soon longed to see her barge in
When restless retirement hours came
And all who were blessed with her tender care
Never forgot her name.

Diagnostic Genius

He had so much money, he used it to start
The fire in his furnace each morn.
He owned six banks, a chain of stores
And sixteen counties of corn.
He developed a cough, and an aching back
He couldn't sleep at night
He'd often shiver, then start to quiver
His bowels were loose, his chest was tight.

They called in doctors from over the world
They even tried to Faith Heal.
They ran countless tests, with equipment the best
Diagnosis they failed to reveal.
They treated with liniment, salves and pills
And manipulations galore.
They tried every cure, but were never quite sure
What they were treating for.

Well finally they brought an old Mid-wife in
She said after taking one look
"Tis Aisy fur me, the trouble to see
His stockings are on the wrong foot."

Writer's note:
One has a right and a left on a pair of pants and a right leg in a left leg is almost impossible to conceal,. Try putting the right arm in a left sleeve and you wind up backwards.

Gloves and even mittens have a left and a right; they are truly a pair.
But you can buy a half a dozen pair of black sox and you get twelve identical sox. You can put them on either foot or even at times inside out and one notices little difference. So have I really got 6 pair of sox or just a dozen sox?

The Escape Cure

She never ever cracks a smile
Protruding teeth look like a file
Assigned patients to her care
Know her as a Holy Terror
The worst of pills somehow are nice
Compared to her look of Ice
Baby, child, woman, man
Dread to ask her for the pan
many patients soon get well
To escape—This ward is hell

Cardiac Surgery

Silence
My drug filled brain
Reviews events
Resulting in
My presence here.

Movement—
Hot surgical lights
Piercing eye lids—
Gowned attendants
Everywhere.

A sigh—
A mask descends
Silencing lips—
Whispering—Whispering
A silent prayer.

Consciousness fades
Accepting HEART REPAIR
or OBLIVION
For me lying there.

"OH LORD—MY GOD—"

Well—Maybe

Yesterday I took a walk
Its been three months ago
Since my by-pass surgery
I'm almost healed you know
For days I've sized up this hill
And made myself a bet
Soon I'd be strong enough
To scale that hill—and yet
The doctor said go easy
The nurses say don't strain
But I can hardly bide my time
To try my wings again
But when a man is eighty
And has an eighty heart
He'd best surmise the finish
Before he makes a start.

Conclusion?

"Is there anything left to write about?"
The gray haired poet said
"Is there any message I can impart
Before I'm finally dead?"
"I've penned about the glory of Spring
The picturesqueness of Fall
The beauty of white clad winter
Summer's sunsets and all"

"I've written about those youthful dreams
The memories and wisdom of age
Of Love and Life, of Hate and Strife
My works fill many a page"
"Are these works finally destined?
To a place on a moldering shelf
Will any of this inspire others?
Are my labors only for self?"

No one answered, had no one heard?
But the rustling of leaves and grasses
A haunting echo—A barking dog
And the sighing wind as it passes

Voices

Voices—
Mother's
Bobby's
Wife's
Dead—
Dead these years
NO! NOT NOW

Nurse—NEEDLE—
Vials of blood
Tube—
Draining—
Draining blood?
Voices fading—
Light failing—
STOP! STOP!

Draining—
Raining—
Raining, Draining
Blood—
Silent Draining
Tired—
Blood tired—
Fading—Fading.......

"Now I lay me down to sleep"—
"I fear no evil—"

“E-en though I walk thru the shadow—”
“My soul to keep—”
Forever and ever—”
I FEEL!! I SEE!!
WHO IS THERE?
HELLO? HELLO!!
DAMN YOUR HIDE, HELLO

The Hug Cure

I seek my Doctor
When ever I feel ill
He prescribes a liquid
Or maybe just a pill
Its become quite common
And likely too as not
He'll instruct the Nurse
To give me a shot
But the cure that really matters
The one that makes my day
Is the hug my Nurse gives me
As I go on my way

Nighttime Guardian Angel

Somewhere between
Hallucination, and dreaming
Or in and out of both.
Comes the Lady of Patience
And Mercy

Soft hand brushes a shoulder
Soft the touch, like the brush
Of the wing of an Angel
With voice as soft
She comforts

He kisses the hand surrendering
In complete confidence
To her ministrations
Even to his most intimate needs
His Night time
Guardian ANGEL

Writer's note: Often the personnel in Clinic or Hospital are so busy that patients feel neglected. But there are quiet times when some of the personnel take a few extra minutes with a patient. Those are often never to be forgotten minutes. *This is true be it Head Nurse or House Keeper.*

Twenty-Four-Hour Minutes

At a quarter to five in the morning
Nurse arrived with the morning news
Gave morning medication
And brought her a glass of juice
At six nurse was there with a wash cloth
And towel to freshen her up
She'd asked for hot tea that morning
So they brought her a steaming cup
Nurse said "I'll be back in a minute
To take you into the shower"
She took a look at her wrist watch
Seven o'clock was the hour.
She sat there impatiently waiting
Afraid the shower would be late
And she might possibly miss it
They served her breakfast at eight
At nine they came with a wheel chair
That ride was quite a suprise
To think that she was transported
For a walking exercise
For once there it was out of the wheel chair
To go for a walk and a talk
She thought, "Without that wheel chair
I could already have had my walk"
Back to her room by wheel chair
Served more pills to clear her head
Instead of the shower she was longing for
They promptly put her to bed

Thus she spent the hours of daylight
Anticipating that bath
When she told a nurse how she'd missed it
The night nurse had a good laugh
So she asked the nurse next morning
As she took her tray away
How she had missed that shower
Nurse said, "I was busy all day"
But you're due for a shower this morning
I'll be back in a minute. O. K.?"
I don't know if she got a shower this next day or not.

Writer's note: As a patient one spends most of their time wasting and often minutes do seem like hours. But this was actually a twenty four hour minute.

Admission for Surgery

The day before/with things galore
They packed his pockets and case
With anything loose/even kitchen juice
And Gin hid deep in its place
A song book of blues/the daily news
Fresh socks and underwear
They were ready at seven/and left at eleven
Drove with confidence-care

He enjoyed that ride /by his daughter's side
'Neath the light of the paling moon
They hoped to get there/with minutes to spare
Never dreaming they would get there so soon
The girl at the desk/bad them to rest
The clock their admission controlled
She dared not to start/to work on his chart
'Til the midnight bell had tolled
For Medicare power/chose this witching hour
For a patient that sought admission
So they wouldn't pay/for an extra day
T'was a money saving decision

Soon in thru the door /came several more
Of others to await admissions
Two minutes before/ thru that very same door
Came two for emergency reasons
He was dying of thirst/but these last came first
So time passed allowed for drinking

With a mouth dry as cotton/and a taste that was rotten
He sat there sweating and thinking
At a quarter to two/ they finally got to
Processing the papers they said
He got a night shirt/and in spite of his hurt
Gratefully sank into bed

Then a voice from the deep/stopped him from sleep
With a half hundred more of questions
After having to sign/line after line
They gave him some final suggestions
He looked at his watch/ came to with a start
He was late for his operation!!

A Seemingly Goldberg Invention

I woke at four—an ungodly hour
And waited for help to take a shower
I thought my Doctor was out of his head
When he ordered me into a bath instead
Thinks I if I sit in a tub you'll know
I wasn't chiding, I told you so
That bathroom was as big as a meeting hall
With a lot of weird gadgets along the wall
She stood me on one that hung like a swing
Stripped off my gown and weighed with this thing
Re-draping the gown she had me step clear
Turned me around for a gadget quite near

In the middle of the room, forming a hub
Was a sculpture in porcelain, a gigantic tub
She pushed a button and without a sound
One third of that tub swung out and around
What should appear to my wondering eyes
Was a porcelain seat three times my size
She turned me around and onto that seat
And stripped me of gown again very neat
Placing my feet well off of the floor
She closed that tub like closing a door
It fit very neatly the rest of the tub
And a latch sealed me in as snug as a bug
A fountain of suds rose up at my feet
'Til I sat in suds, up belly deep

She gave me a cloth and I heard her say,
"Clean up your privates the usual way"
I became so involved in this unusual game
I forgot false modesty and felt no shame
Meanwhile she took a cloth from a rack
And proceeded to scrub my torso and back
Then she drained the tub and gave me a spray
To flush from my body the soap suds away
That hand held Bedit worked as smooth as glass
To a hole in the seat I made a good pass
That rinsed off my scrotum and de-soaped my ass
When dry she draped me with that backless gown
With a soothing lotion she rubbed me down
Back in my bed I settled down deep
And dreamed of bathing all day in my sleep.

Health Assistant Honey

Hi there little chatterbox
I met you once before
When you were filling in
On this other floor
At first I thought you flighty
As I watched you here and there
But now I know your secret
You were needed every where
And if you leave un finished
As you scamper out the door
Its because you see a patient
That really needs you more

Aboard the Cataract Bus

It may surprise the first reader this thing about surgical procedure
One takes all tests and are signed to go before they tell you what can happen you know
The driver had gathered patients all in, the Hostess welcomed them all with a grin
We'd been served some goodies and told a few jokes, before
the driver finally spoke
"Now that you are settled get a grip on your chair and I'll tell you about this eye repair.
They dope you up until you're half dead then they strap fast
to a bed
They poke you with a needle again and again until you can
feel almost no pain
Then Doc uses his thumbs and bye and bye out of your head
pops your eye
Before you recover from this little shock he has your eye on
a chopping block
With a knife and a prod and a nurse standing by, he slices and prods into that eye
Once in a while his hand will stay while the nurse mops the
blood away

He spreads open the cut/give the eye a whack out pops the
lens and the old cataract
He forces the new lens in with a fight/then he pokes and he
prods it 'til it is just right
The nurse again mops up the red, Doc pops that eye right
back in your head
Though your face is now black and blue, your eye is back as
good as new
Though you may feel you have really been had Nurse says with
a smile "Now that wasn't so bad
You really don't know how lucky you be if you find that you
still can see"
The bus was quiet as quiet as a mouse/ you could hear a pin
drop any where in the house
The patients all figured Aw what the hell, had their surgery
and things went well

My Friend, the Stranger

I lay there silently watching
As they came and stripped the bed
Now deprived of that personality
The bed was lifeless and cold
Without his robust nature
And memories treasured like gold
I recalled the wee hours of morning
How a bellow loud and deep
Espoused a hearty welcome
To both of us fast asleep
Six oclock would see his mother
Six thirty a Sister dear
A Pal showed up at seven oclock
To bring him a bit of cheer
T'was daughters and sons by ten oclock
And so on through out the day
It was like Grand Central station
About three feet away
Now the bed is empty
I lie there aware of my pain
I don't wish ill for that stranger
But I wish he were back again

CRITTERS AND COWBOYS AND OTHER TALES

The Balladeers

We are the ones who write for fun
Even penning the path of a hearse
Our pages are red with the maimed and the dead
We kill for the sake of the verse.

Our maidens sigh and cry and die
As their pitiful tale is told
there are heroes great who meet with fate
Or their very souls are sold

With a pen we slip the gun from their hip
To give you the wild, wild West
Put a ship to sleep on the ocean deep
And the captain goes down with the rest

Our tales of horror and splashes of gore
page after page after page
Bodies strewn from room to room
By a mother that dies in a rage

There are wild, wild tales of raging gales
And youth returning fountains
Earthquakes snakes and poison lakes
And hot volcanic mountains

To entertain we seek with pain
The reader of today
For even a song if ten lines long
is sure to be cast away.

Harvest in a Bean Field

The day was hot and sultry
The others all had gone
Listlessly she pulled at beans
Of bean row stretching on

She really should not have been there
The baby was due soon
If money weren't so precious
She would have quit at noon

Sometimes one had to do
Things they did not like
The little family had to eat
An Mike was out on strike

Suddenly a stabbing pain
Made the woman yield
And little Mike was born that day
In the dusty field.

An Answer to a Prayer

She felt so old as she knelt in the cold
By her cat in this little place
With one small light
To keep out the night
It barely lit her face

"Oh God" says she, "If I could be
Once more fed and well,
I'd go any place
So's not to face
This cruel and living Hell"

They found her there beside her chair
Her face sort of alight
The final healing to all life's ills
Was granted to her that night.

A M(u)rn(e) In a Farmer's Life

Picture a hopeless farmer, on a bone chilling wet April morn
With a half tamed team and his shattered life
In a rocky field that is only a swamp
And a woman akin to Satan himself

(Pause for Commercial)

The bone-chilling rain reminds him
Of that chilling look of his wife
As he complained of the half cooked bacon
And over cooked egg at breakfast
As he fights to control the half tamed team
He's .reminded of his uncontrollable wife
Who insists on half making the bed
Where he lies sleepless in a lumpy tangle of sheets
The rocky swampy field reminds him
Of his wife's soggy, lumpy bread
And those chilling-remarks as
he sought to steal a feel
In bed on that chilly morning

(Pause for Commercial)

Wind sweeps the mist drizzle clouds apart
The sun bursts through, warming him to the bone
The raucous team has settled to a steady walk
Is there hope that he will one day drain the swamp
And clear the rocks from the soil?
Is there hope he will one day clear
That rocky marriage path?

Oh Lord My God, is there hope for the hopeless one?
"This is your cheerful announcer
Announcing the conclusion of another episode in
"THE LIFE OF A FARMER", And now
A Word from Our Sponsor"

Cowboy Heaven

They say there's a Cowboy heaven
Where the singing Cowboys go
They are joined by Cowboy Poets
And performers of radio
Cowboy singers of the talkies
Roy Rogers and Autrery are there
With the Sons of the Pioneers
In the cowboy garb they wear
Guitars and Mouth Organs are provided
And even a mouth harp or two
The air is alive with musical Ballads
Occasionally a poem or two
Fiddlers are present with Fiddles
That are kept in tune on hand
To play that square dance music
Maybe even a kitchen band
A circuit riding preacher
Presides over the happy throng
And Angels smile as they listen
To praises of God in song
There's campfire and bunkhouse humor
Stew and coffee are free
I just hope there's a place in the shadows
For minor Poets like me.

Livestock Beware

Mike was just a saddle tramp
He followed the Rodeo game
In bars he took his whiskey neat
In time he made a name
He boasted, "There just Ain't no critter
That stands on four legs or two
On wheels skis or by propeller
That won't do what I want it to"

One night they discovered this Motor Bike
Big, ugly and black
That had put a man in the Hoosegow
This Bike was parked out back
That night with some of the boys liquored up
They came upon this Bike
"Let's see you tame this critter"
Says one of the boys to Mike

Says Mike, "I'll tame this critter
Before the coming sun
He straddled that contraption
And gave the gas the gun
A trail of smoke was the last they saw
But the valley was filled with the roar
It's path led through a haystack
A water tank and barndoor

Two cows forever quit grazing
A flock of sheep ended in two
It was simply amazing
What Mike and that Bike could do
There are pieces of that Motor Bike
Strewn over Hill and Dale
And Mike is convalescing
In the local County Jail
Trying to round his bail up
His saddle is up for sale

It Was Bound to Happen

Only 4'6" Jeremiah Hicks, was age thirty six
Before he chose to mix
With a lady of the town
Angela Ballau, was all of 6'2"
Always dressed in blue
Shoes and gown
A quite unusual pair, him away down there
And she up in the air
But they chose by wedding to be bound
Her breasts were deep and wide when he kissed the bride
His head got stuck inside of
Her gown.

Freelance Nance

In a house of sin/ and sex and Gin
Where on eyed Jacks were wild
In the midst of a flight/ one Saturday night
Was born this half breed child
Un unclad feet/ through the dusty street
She roamed about the town
People swore/ she'd be a whore
Peddling flowers/ in the day light hours
She managed to save and eat
How only God knows/ she bought fine clothes
And left the life of the street
She haunted the star/ a restaurant and bar
Hustled drinks/ from country hicks
And cowboys from afar
Her voice was low and sultry/ as was her evening gown
Though her life was hazardous/ it never got her down
It was only natural that at an early age
She ceased to work at the tavern/ to act upon the stage
Many a city Dandy came calling at her door
In spite of style or riches/ they all failed to score
Finally she met an actor/ who her head soon turned
But the cad proved unfaithful/ and her love was spurned
This is this story's moral/ you get what you have earned
Those who play with fire/ eventually will get burned.

Wanda Willow Wilson

Wanda Willow Wilson/born in a music store
Studied voice and music/before the age of four
Her voice was so enchanting/at the age of five
They gathered just to hear her sing/she kept the store alive
With the lead in Madam Butterfly/at the tender age of nine
She dressed in fancy opera clothes/never missed a line
She practiced in the open fields/made the tall corn grow
Performing at the County Fair/she made the roosters crow
They billed her into Carnegie Hall/ the place was filled that night
Dressed up to do her numbers/she really was a sight
With bouncy boobs a bursting/and corset oh so tight
Before one note from orchestra/there was a clarion blast
As our heroin gave a little cough/and her gas she passed
The place was filled the next night/they must have been insane
To think that she would stand up there/and do the same again.

Sloe Eyed Pearl

Somewhere between Morden and Caspen/ if you follow an ancient trail
You will find a deserted home stead/ where frequently the wind reaches a Gail
The out buildings are nothing but rubble/ the corral is no longer in use
That once confined a milk cow/ a goat and a sway backed cayuse

The roof of the cabin has sagged in/ long gone are the windows and door
The joists are completely rotted away/ that used to support the floor
This once was the home of a sodbuster/a circuit preacher who rode far and wide

To marry and to baptize children/ and save an old sinner's hide
Upon a knoll at the cabin's back/ is an iron fenced in plot
If you search for it in the grass and weeds/ You'll find it likely as not
There lay buried the preacher's wife/ an Uncle and his only son

It is his final resting place/now that his life's work is done
Outside of this fence, but adjacent to it/ are seven in separate grave
Lies the Infamous Sloe Eyed Pearl/ and six of the lives she gave
Sloe Eyed Pearl thus has company/ for her molding bones

For surrounding her in a U shape are six of the seven tombstones
In the first is her eldest son Jacob/who was drowned one early spring
Then John who was the second born/ on stage he would dance and sing
Next, June the blue eyed beauty/with a mass of golden curls

Then Jean, and Joan and Julie/ the other three of her girls
Thus with her was six of her flock/all candidates for heaven
For they had led exemplary lives/ all six of the seven
She had gained them all without wedlock/ when she worked in the town dance hall

Where she had made a fortune/ answering to man's call
In spite of her trade and her life of shame/ she had morally raised her flock
To become useful citizens/ in the neighboring town of Black Rock
The old Sodbusting Preacher had willed this spot/for pearl and six of her clan

Who proved to be jewels in their mother's crown/ a model for struggling man
You might wonder why this preacher willed/ this plot as he had done
Unbeknownst to the populous, he was the seventh/he was her other son.

The Tale of Sandy Ed McPhail

This cowboy Sandy Ed McPhail road alone an endless trail
In scorching sun or rain and hail
To find the Cat house of his dreams
One night the stars were bright, he saw a city all alight
Decided there he would spend the night
Perchance in the Cat house of his dreams

Chorus

Where some were tall and some were lean
And some were sort of in between
Some were small and some were plump
And some were heavy in the rump

He rubbed his pony down, spread his blanket on the ground
And dreamed of going into town
To that Cathouse of his dreams
He drank his way with Whiskey raw, in a bar until he saw
That Cat house sitting in a draw
That Cat house of his dreams

Chorus

A house a four story high each window had a bright red eye
This was the place his throat went dry
T'was the Cat house of his dreams
The door alight was open wide, he doffed hat, stepped inside
To seek some Damsel by his side
In this Cat house of his dreams

Chorus

He made his way to every floor, and each and every door
To find this very special whore
In this Cathouse of his dreams
Some had hair a snowy white, some had hair as black as night
Some wore wigs that looked a sight
In this Cat house of his dreams

Chorus

Sloe eyed girls, bedroom eyes, some with beauty otherwise
But none could make his passion rise
In this Cathouse of his dreams
With a chill he awoke, a stiff and lonely old cowpoke
It seems that dream was just a joke
Of that Cat house of his dreams

Ugly Alice

She was born in a cattle feedlot/a steer stepped on her face
It rearranged her features/there was hardly a thing in plac e
Her ears were out of level/she was left with a one sided grin
And when she chose to close her mouth/her top teeth touched her chin
When she finally learned to talk/it was with a sort of stutter
As the words passed over her tongue/it flapped with a sort of flutter
She got a job in a slaughter hours/where she acquired her name
She entertained drunken butchers/to whom all girls looked the same
She was industrious and frugal/and to everyone's great surprise
She saved up for a plastic surgeon/and had a doctor rearrange her eyes
For one of them stared eerily at you/while the other roamed the skies
The surgeon leveled her ears up/broke her jaw and re-did her tongue
Braced and reduced her upper teeth/'twas improvement what he had done
But he said, " I am not an eye doctor/perhaps it would be wise

To hire a good eye surgeon/have him re-do you eyes."
She filed the appropriate papers/and after considerable delay
She was assigned a contract surgeon/and eagerly awaited the day
The doctor who was assigned to attend her/didn't mind the eye firm in her face
But the other eye gave him the willies/as it roamed all over the place
The nurse put a patch on that orbit/while doc got his tools in place
He proceeded to probe slice and sculpture/that untouched part of her face
He instilled in that eye some movement/and to his great surprise
He managed by manipulation/to give her a bedroom eye.

Barney's Lament

On the fist day of marriage my Katy served to me
A big boiled rooster with Dumplings floating
And a cup of fragrant English tea

The second day of marriage my Katy served to me
A delicious beef roast,
And bits of boiled rooster with dumplings floating free

The third day of marriage my Katy served to me
A succulent leg of lamb, delicious roast beef
And bits of boiled rooster with dumplings floating free

The fourth day of marriage my Katy served to me
A Virginia baked ham, a succulent leg of lamb, a delicious beef roast
And bits of boiled roaster with dumplings floating free

On the fifth day of marriage my Katy served to me
A stuffing stuffed salmon, a Virginia baked ham, a succulent leg of lamb, a delicious beef roast
And bits of boiled rooster with Dumplings floating free

On the sixth day of marriage my Katy served to me
A huge pot of Goulash, a big stuffed salmon, a Virginia baked ham, a succulent leg of lamb, a delicious beef roast
And bits of boiled rooster with dumplings floating free

The seventh day of marriage my Katy served to me
Cheese and macaroni, a huge pot of Goulash, a stuffing stuffed salmon, a Virginia baked ham,
A succulent leg of lamb, a delicious beef roast, and bits of boiled rooster with dumplings floating free

For the next six weeks my Katy served to me
All the leftovers that she hadn't served to me

A Day Best Forgotten

They both agreed there was no need
To 'fess up 'bout the past
For he had been a Sailor
And she notoriously fast
The diamond that he gave her
Had been worn before
An often resized ring
For fingers a full score
She wore the same wedding dress
That had been her pride
For six or seven nuptials
Where she had been a bride
In their fancy dresser
Were three giant drawers
One was his and one was hers
And one considered ours
One day when she was shopping
He saw this rosewood box
With a little hasp and hinges
Absent any locks
When he first observed it
He could only stare
Was it for a purpose
That she had left it there?

Temptation overcame his vow
He flipped aside the clasp
And there before him lay
A road into her past
Neatly nestled one on one
Were letters tied in blue
He could not resist to read
As some of us might do
There was no date or signature
But it was plain to see
There had been torrid passion
In nights beside the sea

She found him on a straight chair
With letters everywhere
She put them back into the box
Said Darling cant you see
Those are the torrid letters
That you once wrote to me
He smiled then as he recalled
On nights by cabin light
He had dictated to a friend
Because he couldn’t write

Dizzy Daisy the Doodler

She drew designs with her dinner / when she was less than two
She played with chalk and crayons / as girls with dollies do
Her nursery walls were a giant maze / of curves and scrawls and lines
She drew the weirdest patterns / thought provoking designs

The teachers could not read her work / her penmanship a mess
For what she scribbled on each page / was anybody's guess
She finger painted sister / and that was such a sight
That it caused her baby brother / to lay screaming in the night

She drew a map for her boyfriend / that was such a maze
The first time that he used it / he was lost for days
Now when you try to follow them / you may think perhaps
That Daisy the Dizzy Doodler / draws Rand McNally maps

Red Light District of Before

These are the days when one looks back
Of the Red Light District by the railroad track
Where girls got proficient in the oldest trade
And a boy discovered how babies were made

An Indian girl known as Willowy Duck
Half starved and really down on her luck
Decided to earn the old fashioned way]
Entertain young boys for fun and for pay

Her very first customer behind the Red Light
Decided to stay and pay all the night
He was young and virile and a handsome boy
Their activities brought them both so much joy

When they had finished she rose and she smiled
Knowing they both had had their fill
She accepted from him her very first pay
The customary two dollar bill

Each Saturday night he came to play
She was always happy and gay
Though she'd collected that very first day
She never from him accepted more pay

He was called to war and left before
He had that last chance to return to her door
When he returned, the war being o'er
He found her house wasn't there any more

Many a year had passed away
When a mailman delivered a letter one day
It contained a woman's attested last will
It simply said "I loved you Will!"
And contained therein a two dollar bill.

An Unforgettable Performance

Dolly Paige
Took to the stage in the days of Vaudeville
She could dance or sing
Or any thing, frequently brought down the hall
She could play Juliet
And the French Florette
And even the little flower girl
She could recite Dan McGrew
And the Gal known as Lou
She even gave opera a whirl

Now Dangerous Dan
Was her leading man
With a mustache or full whiskered grin
He had once played Hamlet
And had run the gambit
Of Shakespeare when Shakespeare was in

T'was a hot sultry night
And the stage was alight
With only the moon and a star
The old music man
Played as Music men can
Ending with one crashing bar

Now Dangerous Dan
The leading man spent the day at the Inn Drinking toasts
To heroes and Ghosts
With Lime that was well laced with Gin
Though sure of feet
And dressed very neat
He chose to ignore his lines

Instead of a sneer
Or a villainous leer
He knelt to a poor girl distressed
And gave a show
Of Romeo
As her golden locks he caressed

Dolly responded with bits of Opera
Their acting was really a sight
Though it seemed weird
The audience cheered
And gave a standing Ovation that night

When asked the next day about the play
They seemed to agree in the main
That it was about
A lady quite stout
And a Villain who had gone quite insane

Bernie the Houseboat Rabbit

See that Rabbit over there
Not running, jumping everywhere
But happily grazing grass with care
It's Bernie the Houseboat Bunny

He doesn't act the Rabbit way
Sitting still and scared each day
Instead he is content to play
Bernie the Houseboat Bunny

His Mistress takes him out each day
Upon a leash so he won't stray
He doesn't know another way
Bernie the Houseboat Bunny

I would gladly wear his string
Be cuddled like a precious thing
And have my Mistress softly sing
Like Bernie the Houseboat Bunny

I'd give up without a fight
To have her cuddle me each night
I'd snuggle up to her real tight
Like Bernie the Houseboat Bunny

And if that Rabbit girl was true
We just might do what Rabbits do
And soon there'd be more than two
To cuddle Bernie the Bunny

Note: On a trip with a travel group we saw a lady with a rabbit on a leash. She told me that the rabbit had been raised on a houseboat and never left it except on a leash. It was the most cuddly rabbit I have ever seen.

The Extraction

Off set Sam had a three toe'd foot / walking made him waddle
You would never notice this / when he was in the saddle
It wasn't this, it was a tooth / that made him feel not well
Night and day a cavity / ached to give him hell
He tried a string and door knob / but when he slammed the door
It yanked him from a kitchen chair / and sprawled him on the floor

"Tooth Extraction, night or day", read this swinging sign
All of this done painlessly" / Sam said this for mine
"It's the time that causes pain", said the Tooth Extractor
"I have found a simple way / to correct this factor
I wire a wire securely 'round / your rotten painful member
Then wire it to my bull whip tip / Now remember
Open wide your mouth / don't watch what I'm about
I merely crack this old bull whip / Eureka—tooth is out"
Sam closed his eyes, heard a crack, and landed on his back
The job was done, a tooth / lay glistening in the sun
Then Sam felt the pain return / they'd pulled the wrong darn one

First Choice Is Not Always the Best

Tess was a rancher's daughter / born in the western wild
He sent her to an Eastern school to groom his precious child
His heart was set on using her to gain himself a son
He choose the men to court her she had to choose just one
He choose
Her eastern banker boy friend; the foreman of his ranch
And because he owned another ranch, He gave young Joe a chance
He brought the two outsiders for a two months stay
So she could size them all up and choose the one to stay
The banker brought Donna, his sister she was pretty and loved to play
She flirted with the foreman and stole his heart away
Tess chose the banker, perhaps because of his wealth
That meant a lot more to her than his looks or health
Now Tess is a constant nagger, Donna is never content
Joe is a rich old bachelor, pleased with the way that things went

The Rabbit Rancher

Now Joe was an Oregon Rancher, he had a four acre spread
Four pigs, three goats and five chickens, cattle he had ten head.
Ranching is tough on four acres, pickings for stock is mean
They stamp out grass in spring time, before it has gotten green.

He took a job in a sawmill, worked his eight hours a day
Spent all the funds he had extra, on small grain and tons of hay
He traded his goats for some rabbits, very rapidly they did multiply
He sold to the local butcher, and learned how a rabbit to fry

Now rabbits are not only fertile, they generously fertilize
He planted a two acre garden, his vegetables were a prize

Soon rabbits took place of the cattle, the chickens and all of the swine
He became a Rabbit Rancher, increased his acreage ten times
His Rabbit Boys replaced the cowboys, with shot guns they road the field
The rabbits steadily gained on them, richly increasing his yield

In time he built a packing house, packed Rabbits galore
Sold them across the nation, From Pacific to Atlantic shore
Now some still call him a farmer, because he started so small
But he is known by Oregon Ranchers, as the richest Rancher of all

Adventures in Parenting

A winding cow path led the way
To that special knoll
That had its top removed
And thus create a hole
Where sand and gravel were removed to mix into cement
That went to build foundations
Or floor for basement went

'Twas in this little sheltered place
With a neighbor girl I'd play
We two would make like Mom and Dad
Act in a family way
But sister Sue spied on us
Couldn't wait to tell
What she told our families
Caused all kinds of hell

But when it all was sorted out
They sure could not blame me
For I was only twelve years old
And she was twenty three

Tit for Tat?

Johnny was a day nurse
lou 'May worked at night
At the local hospital
They were man and wife

Now Jimmy was a poet
One night they brought him in
He'd been a car crash
That night when full of Gin

May became his Angel
He had the poet's curse
Instead of speaking openly
He penned it out in verse

Johnny found this fools cap
Copied it for fun
Sent it to the paper
the local daily "Sun"

He found this quite amusing
Nursed this little whim
As the paper published it
With a byline "TIM"

And at last the truth will out
As often does in life
While Johnny stole his poetry
Jimmy stole his wife

Extreme Constipation

One eyed Slim got drunk one night, and got his innards plugged up tight
He'd had that trouble times before/spent hours behind a Privy door
But this time tho with many a groan he could not bring that feces home
He'd had this problem for a week he hurt so bad he could not speak
Then one night to Bud and Jim confided what was wrong with him
"Eat lots of beans" Bud did say/"the beans will blast the plug away"
They only gave him violent cramps/ and a putrid odor in his pants
At last Slim told the Ranch house cook/ who checked the recipes in his book
Not one recipe made Old Slim pass/ from Prunes to boiled Chickweed grass.
Now there was this China man so weird/that he'd even comb and part his beard
Some said he'd studied ills one time/ sort of like a doctor's line
This yellow man chewed on his Que/ said there's a way that you can do
This thing that you are fixen to
"Get a gallon Grease drum or better three/and hang it in that big Oak tree

Fill it with water warm as rain/with soap enough to ease the pain
Make a siphon with a hose/you know where the free end goes"
They hung that drum high in the tree/the cowboys hung around to see
How soapy water wet and warm/could make Ol'Slim's bowels perform
Jim with the hose the opening found/on Slim's behind there on the ground
Bud says it probably will be tough/to know when Slim has had enough.
Ten whole minutes water found/Its way into Slim on the ground
Then suddenly Slim shakes loose the hose/there is a blast and he goes and goes
Til Bud says there's no way to win/un less we drive a bung plug in
There was ten acres of new hay/ that Slim fertilized that day/
For that the boss gave extra pay/ but who would want to earn this way
The moral you should think about/ What you take in you must let out.

Shades of Leap Year

Leap Year it's a fact as every one knows
A lady may choose herself to propose
John and Edith weren't children/
He was fifty and she was forty five
They had been keeping company
Since the year she was twenty five
She decide it was time to quit waiting
For John to break down and ask
She decided to take the bit in her teeth
If he couldn't she'd take the task
She composed a lengthy proposal
Recalling events of the years
Those pleasant days of courtship
Even recalling some of the tears
She cooked his favorite dinner
Served him his favorite wine
Then she brought to him his slippers
As he sat in his favorite chair
Then kneeling she read her proposal
She ended it with a prayer
Then she paused to await an answer
And suddenly started to weep
Thru her epic and with a full stomach
John sat there fast asleep

The Lone Farm Cowhand

I've often heard my mother say/ I was conceived on a rainy day/ in our old cow barn up in the hay
In an empty stall before the sun/I was born a scrawny one
My Maw said to her other son/ Take care of your brother 'til the milking's done
I guess that it was only fate/ that whilst my brother slept in late
My Maw would always wake me up/ to go and fetch the cattle up
One day I stepped upon a nail/ and went to mother feeling pale
She used my Granny's certain cure/they soaked my foot in cow manure.
I smelled of silage and cow dung/ I'd been with cow since time begun
Maw sent me to the country school/to learn my sums and golden rule
My teacher said run out and play/I really can not stand the way
My little barn boy smells today/ don't come back another day/unless you've scrubbed that smell away
I learned me many a Cowboy song/and sang to my cows all day long/The notes were very clear and strong/even tho the most were wrong
I met my wife at a county fair/with the smell of cow do every where
In the bright straw we pitched woo/a month went by before we knew/ what it was we'd have to do.

You've guessed it she became my bride/with her champion Jersey by her side
Our wedding picture's was real cool/perched on a tandem milking stool
I've spent much more time I'll allow/than any other with the cow
And I shall probably meet my fate/ with that old bull that I hate
I ask you now GEE WHIZ IF I AIN'T A COW BOY WHO THE HELL IS?

Sister Mary's Little Lamb

We'd bottle fed this little lamb her wool was snowy white
She did every thing with us but sleep with us at night
She soon became a nuisance in every sort of way
Like standing in the cow barn door to shy the cows away
One night when I was milking a big old Holstein cow
That confounded wooly sheep got in the barn somehow
She bumped my pail spilled the milk, the Holstein panicked now
I lost my balance slipped from stool and fell behind that cow
Her hind legs beat a rhythm above it made me wrench
I cursed as I lay sopping wet in that old cow trench
They dragged me from that awful mess ans laughed at how I stank
And they took me out and dumped me in the old stock tank
Maw would not let me in the house until I bathed again
They even brought fresh clothing which I donned in pain
I never saw that sheep again, I asked my mother why
She just changed the subject, my Mother would not lie
But one Sunday dinner we had for Uncle Ham
There upon the table was a juicy Leg of Lamb

The Loves of Lou

Lou was a dance hall lady/with hair the color of cream
She smelled like the flowers of the prairie/she was a Cowboy's dream.
The cowpokes clustered around her/dined her and treated her swell
But if they choose to go farther/she fended them off very well
She was due for comeuppance/she fell for a sheep man's son
Her dance hall career was finished/her heart the shepherd had won
The cowboys no longer did ask her/to drink dine or to sleep
She became a sheep herder's Lambkin/and began to smell like a sheep
He gave her a life on the prairie/in a lonely sheep herder's shack
She longed the lights of the dance hall/and to have her old job back
Along came an old Prospector with gold he lured her away
She vied with his burro for favors/and slaved in his mine each day
Then there was this Sodbuster/he was simple and strong
You'd think with such a fellow/that nothing else could go wrong
Now her life is planting and children/her way is study and sure

As she spends her days at a cook stove/or pitching barn manure
Now girls there is this lesson/one that you ought to know
If you are mean and fickle/true love can lay you low
Cow boys may smell like horses/and miners of whiskey or Gin
But if you choose a sheep man/Your troubles are sure to begin
And men for you there's a lesson/one that you ought to know
It the nature of Dance hall women/to play the field so go slow
They will laugh and dance and tease you/and take you for your shirt
Then off to another flirtation/ leaving you in the dirt
But if you woo the boss's daughter/avoiding a life of sin
You'll work for the old man for nothing/there's no way that you can win

The Plight of the Lonesome Cowboy

His breakfast had been Sow Belly
That was used to flavor the beans
The song in his heart had been stifled
By the aroma that rose from his Jeans
Then his bowels foretold the arrival
Of more than the tumult of gas
He sat real tight in the saddle
Hoping the misery would pass

Show caps were on the Sage brush
And cactus was everywhere
Waiting to prick the unwary
That did not squat with care
He faced a momentous decision
Should he trust this moment to chance
And squat in the Cactus and Sage Brush?
Or carry this home in his pants?

SELECTIONS AT RANDOM

Old Baldy

In a cave three bears were born in the forest green
One was small, one was big, one was in-between
The big bossed the others, grew up proud and bold
The little one was timid, stayed sheltered from the cold

The big one left the others, Far and wide roam
Fought and bluffed his way around, forgotten was his home
Blustering gained him nothing, one day he met a man
That shot at him and killed him while hunting o'er the land

The smallest one too timid grew, lived by fear alone
Nothing of the woods he knew til he was fully grown
He too lost his life one day while crouching back in fear
Trying hard to call for help, this left just one bear.

This bear grew up in hardship, learned to trust his nose
His eyes, his ears, his inner sense, the feel of things to toes
That weary were from hardship and cautious to my friend
Soon he was known as Baldy, the smartest in the glen

Hunters often trailed him when he was on the roam
Baited traps, camped on trails but never found him home
Weary then and footsore, they finally stumbled back
Only to see on a lower trail, Old Baldy's giant track

O’er mountains, ledges, valleys He sought a living fare
While all the trappers sought him but could not trap that bear
He liked the sweetest honey, always got it too
There was a store of knowledge in what Old Baldy knew

To man he taught this lesson, don’t ever be too bold
And yet don’t be too cautious or you may lose your hold
Don’t try to out bluff problems, in the end it won’t work Gents
Just make the best of your knowledge flavored with common sense.

Road to Sacrifice

You laid upon your bunk
With thoughts so far away
Or lit a cigarette
And growled or laughed each day
Lay now lay
In darkness filth and mud
Lay now lay
In rotting flesh and blood

You kissed and courted well
And made sweet maidens sigh
You laughed and joked the one
Who when you left did cry
Kiss now kiss
The stinking earth beneath
Kiss now kiss
A blooming floral wreath

You walked so proud in line
In step with manner grand
And held your head so high
A marching to the band
Tramp now tramp
Through mire and murk and lead
Tramp, Tramp, Tramp
Thru blood and filth til dead

You spoke of love of land

Of glory and of merit
Of honorary plaque
How modestly you'd wear it
Lay no lay
Now that all is done
Lay now lay
A 'rotting in the sun

The Ski Slope

From the cozy comfort of the ski lodge
I gaze on the winter scene
Fresh snow blankets the hillside
And the hollows in between
Tree tops form a border
A fringe of lacy net
Smoky wind clouds scurry
Thus complete the set.

Erect, along the towline
Figures smoothly go
I think of the shooting gallery
They have at fairs you know.
I aim an invisible rifle
And in my fancy's fun
I sight these moving targets
Trying to tilt just one.

Chair cars move like swallows
Above the glistening snow
Some drifting up, some drifting down
Endlessly they go
The knoll is alive with figures
Like an army on attack
That in spite of fallen comrades
Will not be turned back.

I see another hillside
Where figures fall in the snow
Not from the loss of balance
But because of the guns below.

Paul

Spread the gospel, spread the gospel
Cried disciples all
"Organize and purify"
Preached Apostle Paul
Tending, mending Christian flocks
From Caesurae to Gaul.

A flash of steel, an arc descending
The final deed was done
The severed member scarcely bleeding
Stared up at morning sun.
Thought had ceased for brain a dying
In that graying head
Christ on earth had lost a champion
Paul the saint was dead.

The Ways of the Good Old Days

Gone are the shocks in the fields of gold
The lofts filled with musty hay
The country school
The horse and mule
And barefoot boys at play.

And the steamer smoke that rose in the fall
The spreader full of manure
Harness is not
Grindstone forgot
These things of the days that were.

The Doc no longer makes house calls
Tho the roads are now graveled or paved
He has the knowledge
Taught in college
But he lacks the personal ways.

The clerk in the stores no longer helps
Visits and gives advise
You tread the aisle
Unblessed by her smile
She's interested only in price.

I'm not about to fret and shout
About those good old days
But think of it
We lost a bit
When we lost those good old ways.

Acceptance of God's Will

I guess we'd stood for an hour or so
In front of the Pub by the old square
When up the street with face aglow
Came Mike a shouting like I don't know
Happy and drunk without a care.

T'was great to see him now so gay
You'd scarce believe that the night before
Mike had stood there ashen gray
Try'n to fight the tears away
Waiting the word of the coming day
With his wife at death's very door.

Now it was, "come on fellows and have one
Lift them boys and lift them high
Ther's nothing like today's sweet sun
Ther's no fun like today's good fun
Ther's no one like old Mike not one
For a babe's been born to May and I."

Today we stood for an hour or so
In the drizzling rain by the old town square
The procession moved along so slow
Taking Mike's wife to bury you know
Taking both her and the babe by Jo
We felt it was so unfair

But Mike came back, His head was up
he bought the drinks with a tearful eye
Said Mike “Drink up boys, raise the cup
Please don’t think I’m a sodden pup
Let’s drink to the two who are going up
To join God in the sky”

We all had whiskey in our glass
The best that Mike could buy
God bless you Mike you sturdy lad
The best of Christian’s we’ve ever had
A lesson to you and I.

The Joys of Single Parenthood

The rumor's out—they're laying off
Her numb feet ache—she has a cough
They keep her over at the store
Then home to find a dog scratched door
The cat has messed on the kitchen floor
Babe's diaper's wet—so's Buddy's bed
She can not rid this aching head
Its time she put this house to bed.
OH HELL! SHE'S OUT OF CIGARETTES

Hey There

No one seems to listen
To things I have to say
I could settle problems
If things were done my way
My ideas are boundless
I speak of them but
All my friends kind of grin
They think I am a nut

A Pleasant Social Interlude

This is a song to our friends from the south
And the country of Ecuador
Of Chimborago and Catapax
Of beautiful birds and Panama hats,
Of jungles, seashore and sun galore,
Of Incas and Spaniards of days of yore.

This is an ode to these friends of the south
Their openness and their charm,
To halting talk and merry ways
Over goodies served on bounteous trays
Of the greeting kiss and one of farewell
God Bless you all—we wish you well.

Prelude to Life and Love

"There little girl, don't cry"
Your little pets passed on
Bird, cats and Balcazar
An others now are gone
But new life here
Will bring you cheer
Not tears but laughter and song

"There little girl, don't cry"
Though ones you loved pass on
Be not afraid
Though memories fade
They will never quite be gone
The heart forgives
Over the years
The best of us lives on

Though you loose the home
You've always known
And your sweet life
Is filled with strife
You are faced with blow on blow
Remember that strife
Is part of life
Pleasure plus pain is how we grow

The best of your life may soon come by
With love and children asking why
And you will explain the where and why
Of life, so please don't cry

A Cup Uh

The Nordics love the coffee bean
The Latins love the vine
For Nordics it's the coffee pot
For Latins it's the wine
For from the British Isle every day at three
Some one "puts a kettle on" for "a cup uh tea"

When Jerry Buzz bombed cities in 1943
The Limeys kept their chin up in spite of misery
Scarce was the occasion when every day at three
Someone didn't "put the kettle on" to have a "cup uh tea"

Dolly was from Devon, a village by the sea
She loved to walk the countryside; lived to ninety-three
No matter what was happening, every day at three
Dolly "put the kettle on" to have a "a cup uh tea"

The Nordics have Valhalla, the Latins, Peter's Gate
Dolly has this vision, she can hardly wait
To have that rocker up in heaven and every day at three
Pause to "put the kettle on" and have a "CUP UH TEA"

At Ninety-One

Today you chill in the afternoon sun
The thermometer registers eighty-one
You ease yourself into an easy chair
And find yourself permanently implanted there
The teeth you purchased at seventy-five
Roam your mouth as though alive
Your step has receded to an uncertain shuffle
There are aches and pains in various muscles
Yet when all is said and all is done
THANK GOD YOU'RE ALIVE AT NINETY-ONE!

Her Last Day at School

Teacher had been there years before
Jane had passed thru that school door
The school bell had rung at half past eight
BE in your seat by nine or your were late
Order was kept with rigid rules
Breaking them meant time after school
Teacher monitored both work and play
Today was graduation day

Her class had passed their final tests
Jane along with all the rest
A last day program had been done
And ice cream served to everyone
They all gathered 'round teacher's chair
The preacher said a little prayer
You'd think that all would be joy and yet
There wasn't and eye that wasn't wet

ON TEACHER'S LAST DAY AT SCHOOL

My Forgitters Gettin' Better All the Time

I forgit what I am thinking, when I start to speaking
I forgit the month and the day of the week
Gone from my mind is my address and street
My forgitters gettin' better all the time

I sent out invitations a whole month away
For some friends to come and feast and play
But on the time set, I'd had time to forget
They have not forgotten yet, so they say
My forgitters gettin' better all the time

My bills keep a comin every day, every day, I file them away
I haven't paid them yet, I'm hoping they'll forget
But they haven't done that yet
And they are threatening to sue for their pay
My forgitters gettin' better every day

When I was very little, I could recite any poem
I remembered every verse, every line
But now that I'm older my mind is getting colder
My forgitters gettin' better every day

My forgitters gettin' better so they say
My forgitters gettin' better every way
My forgitters gettin' better and better and better
My forgitters gettin' better every day

The Cackle Berry

Of all the foods used to cook
The cackle berry takes the book
Boiled or fried or poached or baked
The food that really takes the cake
That are not enhanced by it's style
From fluffed meringue to Angel Cakes
The cackle berry is what takes the eye
It's also used to make good pie
Hens cackle loud when they are done
Laying these from sun to sun
Cackle, Cackle, Cackle

Oh My

My teeth chatter when I talk
My legs wobble when I walk
I wonder what and where
Has happened to my head of hair
I search for my glasses every morn
I'm glad the bathroom's close to me
When I get that urge from ten to three
I never bend over for a dish or cup
For fear I can't stand back up
My hearing's gone with other things
They say it's just what old age brings
I just can't believe that this is for me
Getting close to ninety three

Eagle Eye Alice

Eagle Eye Alice hated all men
She thought they were filthy and full of sin
She kept a female cook on her ranch
She shunned any critter she saw wearing pants
She did her own hunting for Moose and Bear
She used one for meat, the other to wear
To her foreman she mailed her orders each day
Her cook monthly paid cowboys their pay
Now three fingered Jack rode out there one day
We'll soon find out why he went out that way
A blast of buck shot laid him low
He toppled from saddle and lay in the snow
She wrote to her foeman the following note
"There's a critter up hill, go bury the goat
Curly the foreman was in for surprise
AS he bent to intern him, Jack opened his eyes
"You tell that told woman she wasted her lead
I five pounds heavier, but sure ain't dead"
Curly the foreman was looking quite grey
"If I don't get you buried, there will be Hell to pay"
Jack the gambler says "I took ten to one,
I'd bury Old Alice before I was done
So put up your shovel, in time you will see
Eagle Eye Alice is no match for me"
He kidnapped her cook, just for a day

Just to be sure she was out of the way
He bought a bonnet, a black blouse and skirt
He purchased some candles and a cake from a store
Rode out in a buggy to Alice's door
"I come from the town a very long way
To deliver this cake for your birthday today"
Eagle Eye Alice was extinguished that night
Three of the candles were fused dynamite
Three ranch hands sweated and swore
As they scraped Alice from the walls and floor
For three fingered Jack it was not sweat
HE got filthy rich as he collected his bets.

Birthday Time Again

I'm back again at my writing desk
With litter around until I can't rest
With crumpled sheets upon the floor
As I scribble some lines and discard more
What on earth can I say
That I haven't written another day?
I guess there is a thing or two
But to put them on paper would not do
Without my teeth it is my guess
Kissing you would be a mess
We are too old to paint the town
If I knew the right size I could buy a gown
Flowers just wither in days by heck
So HAPPY BIRTHDAY here is a check

At Ninety and One-Half Years

My store bought teeth no longer fit
I've bone hard calluses where I sit
I seldom get to the local stores
'Cause I don't drive my car any more
My voice with a tune is a growl not a shout
Over and over until I wear it out
What my wife is saying I say "yes dear"
Some times that almost causes a fight
When the "yes dear" answer isn't right
I certainly don't kneel to pray
If I knelt down I might stay that way
People say I don't look my age
But what they don't see could fill a page
But in spite of all this, I can cheer
At ninety plus, I'm still here